SLEEPERS
JOINING
HANDS

ROBERT BLY

SLEEPERS JOINING HANDS

HarperPerennial
A Division of HarperCollins*Publishers*

Acknowledgment is made for permission to reprint the following material:

"Six Winter Privacy Poems" and "Hair" first appeared in *Field*.

"The Turtle" (under the title "Turtle Climbing From a Rock") appeared in *The Massachusetts Review*.

"Water Under the Earth" and "Shack Poem" appeared in *The Iowa Review*.

"In a Mountain Cabin in Norway" (under the title "In a Mountain Cabin in Central Norway") appeared in *The Falcon*.

"Tao Te Ching Running" appeared in *Kayak*.

"Condition of the Working Classes: 1970" (under the title "Anarchists Fainting") appeared in *Harper's Magazine*.

"Pilgrim Fish Heads" (under the title "Pilgrim Settlement") appeared in *Tennessee Poetry Journal*.

"Calling to the Badger" (under the title "The Possibility of New Poetry") first appeared in *Contemporary American Poetry*, edited by Donald Hall and published by Penguin Books in 1962. Copyright © 1962 by Robert Bly. Reprinted by permission.

"The Teeth Mother Naked at Last" was originally published in somewhat different form. Copyright © 1970 by Robert Bly. Reprinted by permission of City Lights Books.

"Leonardo's Secret" is reprinted from *The Morning Glory*, published by Kayak Press, Santa Cruz, California. Copyright © 1969–70 by Robert Bly.

Sections of "Sleepers Joining Hands" first appeared under different titles in *Kayak, Lillabulero,* and *The Lamp in the Spine,* and are reprinted with their permission.

A hardcover edition of this book was published by Harper & Row, Publishers, Inc.

First Harper Colophon edition published 1973. Reissued in 1985. First HarperPerennial edition published 1991.

Designed by Sidney Feinberg

Library of Congress Cataloging-in-Publication Data

Bly, Robert.
　Sleepers joining hands.

　(Harper colophon books)
　I. Title.
[PS3552.L9S6　1985]　　811'.54　　84-48642
ISBN 0-06-090785-1 (pbk.)

For Carolyn

"*Still, the mist in the garden is simple* . . .
old ideas go up
like the pure mist of the meadow . . ."
—C. Bly

Contents

Illustrations

I

Six Winter Privacy Poems

1

About four, a few flakes.
I empty the teapot out in the snow,
      feeling shoots of joy in the new cold.
By nightfall, wind,
the curtains on the south sway softly.

2

My shack has two rooms; I use one.
The lamplight falls on my chair and table
and I fly into one of my own poems—
I can't tell you where—
as if I appeared where I am now,
in a wet field, snow falling.

3

More of the fathers are dying each day.
It is time for the sons.
Bits of darkness are gathering around them.
The darkness appears as flakes of light.

4

Sitting Alone

There is a solitude like black mud!
Sitting in this darkness singing,
I can't tell if this joy
is from the body, or the soul, or a third place.

5

Listening to Bach

There is someone inside this music
who is not well described by the names
of Jesus, or Jehovah, or the Lord of Hosts!

6

When I woke, new snow had fallen.
I am alone, yet someone else is with me,
drinking coffee, looking out at the snow.

The Turtle

How shiny the turtle is, coming out
of the water, climbing the rock, as if
the body inside shone through!
As if swift turtle wings swept out of darkness,
crossed some barriers,
and found new eyes.
An old man falters with his stick.
Later, walkers find holes in black earth.
The snail climbs up the wet trunk glistening
like an angel-flight trailing long black banners.
No one finds the huge turtle eggs
lying inland on the floor of the old sea.

Water Under the Earth

O yes, I love you, book of my confessions,
when the swallowed begins to rise from the earth again,
and the deep hungers from the wells.
So much is still inside me, like cows eating in a collapsed strawpile
all winter to get out.
Everything we need now is buried,
it's far back into the mountain,
it's under the water guarded by women.
These lines themselves are sunk to the waist in the dusk under the
          odorous cedars,
each rain will only drive them deeper,
they will leave a faint glow in the dead leaves.
You too are weeping in the low shade of the pine branches,
you feel yourself about to be buried too,
you are a ghost stag shaking his antlers in the herony light—
what is beneath us will be triumphant
in the cool air made fragrant by owl feathers.

I am only half-risen,
I see how carefully I have covered my tracks as I wrote,
how well I brushed over the past with my tail.

I enter rooms full of photographs of the dead.
My hair stands up
as a badger crosses my path in the moonlight.

I see faces looking at me in the shallow waters
where I have thrown them down.
Mother and father pushed into the dark.
That shows how close I am to the dust that fills the cracks on the ocean
    floor,
how much I love to fly alone in the rain,
how much I love to see the jellyfish pulsing at the cold borders of the
    universe.

I have piled up people like dead flies between the storm window and
    the kitchen pane.
So much is not spoken!
I stand at the edges of the light, howling to come in.
Then, I follow the wind through open holes in the blood—
So much ecstasy. . . .
long evenings when the leopard leaps up to the stars,
and in an instant we understand all the rocks in the world.
And I am there, prowling like a limp-footed bull outside the circle of
    the fire,
praying, meditating,
full of energy, like a white horse, saddled, alone on the unused fields.

There is a consciousness hovering under the mind's feet,
advanced civilizations under the footsole,
climbing at times up on a shoelace!
It is a willow that knows of water under the earth,
I am a father who dips as he passes over underground rivers,
who can feel his children through all distance and time!

Shack Poem

1

I don't even know these roads I walk on,
I see the backs of white birds.
Whales rush by, their teeth ivory.

2

Far out at the edge of the heron's wing,
where the air is disturbed by the last feather,
there is the Kingdom. . . .

3

Hurrying to brush between the Two Fish,
the wild woman flies on . . .
blue glass stones a path on earth mark her going.

4

I sit down and fold my legs. . . .
The half dark in the room is delicious.
How marvelous to be a thought entirely surrounded by brains!

In a Mountain Cabin in Norway

I look down the mountainside. Just below my window
several grasses growing raggedly together.

The noise of the snowfed river
winds into the ear, far back into the head.
At three A.M. the big peaks are still lit.

I look over to the other mountainside.
So many pines the eye can't count them!
Sparks of darkness float around me.
No one comes to visit us for a week.

·

Hair

The doctor arrives to inject the movie star against delirium tremens.
Hands that lay so often calm on the horse's mane are shaking.
His hair hangs down like a skier's hair after a fall.
From a whirlpool, drops of black water fly up
and thousands and thousands of years go by,
like an infinite procession of walnut shells. . . .

All that hair that fell to the floors of barbershops over thirty years
lives on after death,
and those shoelaces, shiny and twisted, that we tossed to the side,
gather in the palace of death;
the roarer comes,
the newly dead kneel, and a tip of the lace sends them on into fire!

But the hair weeps,
because hair does not long for immense states,
hair does not hate the poor,
hair is merciful,
like the arch of night under which the juvenile singer lolls back
        drunk. . . .

The Defense Secretary throws his clothes on the floor, and demands to
        be killed,
and flocks of birds turn back in the air, the calf is drawn up into the
        mother's womb,
the scaly tail swirls the muddy water as he turns to leave.

All those men who cannot find the road,
vho die coughing particles of black flesh onto neighboring roofs.
Jailheads that have been brooding on Burton's *Melancholy* under Bal-
        timore rowhouses
roll out in the street, underneath tires,
and catch the Secretary of State
as he goes off to threaten the premiers of underdeveloped nations.

All those things borne down by the world,
corpses pulled down by years of death,
veins clogged with flakes of sludge,
mouths from which bats escape at death,
businessmen reborn as black whales sailing under the Arctic ice . . .

But hair is overflowing with excitable children,
it is a hammock on which the sleeper lies,
dizzy with the heat and the earth's motion,
ecstatic waters, Ordovician hair,
hair that carries the holy, shouting, to the other shore.

In a bureau drawer there are tiny golden pins full of the glory of God—
their faces shine with power
like the cheekbones of saints radiant in their beds
or their great toes that light the whole room!

But Prince Philip becomes irritable, the royal sports car
shoots down the narrow roads,
Judy Garland is led hysterical to the Melbourne plane,
the general joins the Jehovah's Witnesses.

And the Stalinist shoves the papers to the floor,
the priest is unable to go on with the Mass,
the singer tries to climb out through the porthole,
there are broken pieces of wood all around the Jesuit,
the log raft breaks up as it nears the falls,
the spider runs quickly up the blinding path

Under the ground the earth has hair cathedrals
the priest comes down the aisle wearing caterpillar fur.
In his sermons the toad defeats the knight

The dying man waves his son away.
He wants his daughter-in-law to come near
so that her hair will fall over his face.

The senator's plane falls in an orchard in Massachusetts.
And there are bitter places, knots
that leave dark pits in the sawdust,
the nick on the hornblade through which the mammoth escapes. . . .

Tao Te Ching Running

If we could only not be eaten by the steep teeth,
if we could only leap like the rough marble into the next world,
if the anteater that loves to rasp its tongue over the rough eggs of the
    lizard
could walk into a room the carpenters have just left,
or if the disturbed county commissioners could throw themselves like
    a waved hand up into the darkness,
if the fragments in the unconscious would grow big as the beams in
    hunting lodges,
then the tiny black eggs the salmon lays in the luminous ears of nuns
    would be visible,
then we would find holy books in our beds,
then the *Tao Te Ching* would come running across the field!

Condition of the Working Classes: 1970

You United States, frightened by dreams of Guatemala,
building houses with eight-mile-long wings to imprison the Cubans,
eating a bread made of the sound of sunken buffalo bones,
drinking water turned dark by the shadow of Negroes.
You remember things seen when you were still unable to speak—
white wings lying in a field.
And when you try to pass a bill,
long boards fly up, suddenly,
in Nevada,
in ghost towns.

You wave your insubstantial food timidly in the damp air.
You long to return to the shell.
Even at the start Chicago was a place where the cobblestones
got up and flew around at night,
and anarchists fainted as they read *The Decline and Fall*.
The ground is soaked with water used to boil dogs.

Your sons dream they have been lost in kinky hair,
no one can find them,

neighbors walk shoulder to shoulder for three days,
but your sons are lost in the immense forest.

And the harsh deer drop,
the businessmen climb into their F-4s,
the chocks are knocked out,
the F-4 shoots off the deck,
                    trailing smoke,
dipping slightly,
                    as if haunted by the center of the ocean,
then pulling up again, as Locke said it would.

Our spirit is inside the baseball rising into the light

So the crippled ships go out into the deep,
sexual orchids fly out to meet the rain,
        the singer sings from deep in his chest,
memory stops,
                    black threads string out in the wind,
the eyes of the nation go blind.

The building across the street suddenly explodes,
wild horses run through the long hair on the ground floor.
Cripple Creek's survivors peer out from an upper-story window, blood
        pours from their ears,
the Sioux dead sleep all night in the rain troughs on the Treasury
        Building.

The moonlight crouches over the teen-ager's body thrown from a car

The weeping child like a fish thrown from the herring block
the black-nosed Avenger leaping off the deck

Women who hear the cry of small animals in their furs
and drive their cars at a hundred miles an hour into trees

Calling to the Badger

We are writing of Niagara, and the Huron squaws,
the chaise longue, periwinkles in a rage like snow,
Dillinger like a dark wind.
Intelligence, cover the advertising men with clear water,
and the factories with merciless space,
so the strong-haunched woman
by the blazing stove of the sun, the moon,
may come home to me, sitting on the naked wood
in another world, and all the Shell stations
folded in a faint light.

You feel a sadness,
a sadness that rises from the death of the Indians,
from the death of Logan, alone in the house,
and the Cherokees forced to eat the tail of the Great Bear.
We are driven to Florida like Geronimo—
and the young men are still calling to the badger
and the otter, alone on the mountains of South Dakota.

Pilgrim Fish Heads

It is a Pilgrim village; heavy rain is falling.
Fish heads lie smiling at the corners of houses.
Inside, words like "Samson" hang from the rafters.
Outdoors the chickens squawk in woody hovels,
yet the chickens are walking on Calvinist ground.
The women move through the dark kitchen, their heavy
skirts bear them down like drowning men.
Upstairs beds are like thunderstorms on the bare floor,
leaving the covers always moist by the rough wood.
And the eggs! Strange, white, perfect eggs!
Eggs that even the rain could not move,
white, painless, with tails even in nightmares.
And the Indian, damp, musky, asking for a bed.
The Mattapoiset is in league with rotting wood,
he has made a conspiracy with the salamander,
he has made treaties with the cold heads of fishes.
In the grave he does not rot, but vanishes into water.
The Indian goes on living in the rain-soaked stumps.
This is our enemy, this is the outcast,
the one from whom we must protect our nation,
the one whose dark hair hides us from the sun.

The Teeth Mother Naked at Last

I

Massive engines lift beautifully from the deck.
Wings appear over the trees, wings with eight hundred rivets.

Engines burning a thousand gallons of gasoline a minute sweep over
the huts with dirt floors.

The chickens feel the new fear deep in the pits of their beaks.
Buddha with Padma Sambhava.

Meanwhile, out on the China Sea,
immense gray bodies are floating,
born in Roanoke,
the ocean on both sides expanding, "buoyed on the dense marine."

Helicopters flutter overhead. The death-
bee is coming. Super Sabres
like knots of neurotic energy sweep
around and return.
This is Hamilton's triumph.
This is the advantage of a centralized bank.
B-52s come from Guam. All the teachers
die in flames. The hopes of Tolstoy fall asleep in the ant heap.
Do not ask for mercy.

Now the time comes to look into the past-tunnels,
the hours given and taken in school,
the scuffles in coatrooms,
foam leaps from his nostrils,
now we come to the scum you take from the mouths of the dead,
now we sit beside the dying, and hold their hands, there is hardly time
      for good-bye,
the staff sergeant from North Carolina is dying—you hold his hand,
he knows the mansions of the dead are empty, he has an empty place
inside him, created one night when his parents came home drunk,
he uses half his skin to cover it,
as you try to protect a balloon from sharp objects. . . .

Artillery shells explode. Napalm canisters roll end over end.
800 steel pellets fly through the vegetable walls.
The six-hour infant puts his fists instinctively to his eyes to keep out
      the light.
But the room explodes,
the children explode.
Blood leaps on the vegetable walls.

Yes, I know, blood leaps on the walls—
Don't cry at that—
Do you cry at the wind pouring out of Canada?
Do you cry at the reeds shaken at the edge of the sloughs?
The Marine battalion enters.
This happens when the seasons change,
This happens when the leaves begin to drop from the trees too early
"Kill them: I don't want to see anything moving."
This happens when the ice begins to show its teeth in the ponds
This happens when the heavy layers of lake water press down on the
      fish's head, and send him deeper, where his tail swirls slowly,
      and his brain passes him pictures of heavy reeds, of vegetation
      fallen on vegetation. . . .
Hamilton saw all this in detail:

"Every banana tree slashed, every cooking utensil smashed, every mattress cut."

Now the Marine knives sweep around like sharp-edged jets; how beautifully they slash open the rice bags,
the mattresses . . .
ducks are killed with $150 shotguns.

Old women watch the soldiers as they move.

II

Excellent Roman knives slip along the ribs.

A stronger man starts to jerk up the strips of flesh.

"Let's hear it again, you believe in the Father, the Son, and the Holy Ghost?"

A long scream unrolls.

More.

"From the political point of view, democratic institutions are being built in Vietnam, wouldn't you agree?"

A green parrot shudders under the fingernails.
Blood jumps in the pocket.
The scream lashes like a tail.

"Let us not be deterred from our task by the voices of dissent. . . ."

The whines of the jets
pierce like a long needle.

As soon as the President finishes his press conference, black wings carry
       off the words,
bits of flesh still clinging to them.

            *   *   *

The ministers lie, the professors lie, the television lies, the priests
       lie. . . .
These lies mean that the country wants to die.
Lie after lie starts out into the prairie grass,
like enormous caravans of Conestoga wagons. . . .

And a long desire for death flows out, guiding the enormous caravans
       from beneath,
stringing together the vague and foolish words.
It is a desire to eat death,
to gobble it down,
to rush on it like a cobra with mouth open

It's a desire to take death inside,
to feel it burning inside, pushing out velvety hairs,
like a clothes brush in the intestines—

This is the thrill that leads the President on to lie

            *   *   *

Now the Chief Executive enters; the press conference begins:
First the President lies about the date the Appalachian Mountains rose.
Then he lies about the population of Chicago, then he lies about the
       weight of the adult eagle, then about the acreage of the Ever-
       glades

He lies about the number of fish taken every year in the Arctic,
       he has private information about which city *is* the capital of
       Wyoming, he lies about the birthplace of Attila the Hun.

He lies about the composition of the amniotic fluid, and he insists
      that Luther was never a German, and that only the
      Protestants sold indulgences,

That Pope Leo X *wanted* to reform the church, but the "liberal ele-
      ments" prevented him,
that the Peasants' War was fomented by Italians from the North.

And the Attorney General lies about the time the sun sets.

     *   *   *

These lies are only the longing we all feel to die.
It is the longing for someone to come and take you by the hand to
      where they all are sleeping:
where the Egyptian pharaohs are asleep, and your own mother,
and all those disappeared children, who used to go around with you in
      the rings at grade school. . . .

Do not be angry at the President—he is longing to take in his hand
the locks of death hair—
to meet his own children dead, or unborn. . . .
He is drifting sideways toward the dusty places

III

This is what it's like for a rich country to make war
this is what it's like to bomb huts (afterwards described as "structures")
this is what it's like to kill marginal farmers (afterwards described as
      "Communists")

this is what it's like to watch the altimeter needle going mad

*Baron 25, this is 81. Are there any friendlies in the area? 81 from 25,
negative on the friendlies. I'd like you to take out as many structures
as possible located in those trees within 200 meters east and west of my
smoke mark.*

diving, the green earth swinging, cheeks hanging back, red pins blossoming ahead of us, 20-millimeter cannon fire, leveling off, rice fields shooting by like telephone poles, smoke rising, hut roofs loom up huge as landing fields, slugs going in, half the huts on fire, small figures running, palm trees burning, shooting past, up again; . . . blue sky . . . cloud mountains

This is what it's like to have a gross national product.

It's because the aluminum window shade business is doing so well in the United States that we roll fire over entire villages
It's because a hospital room in the average American city now costs $90 a day that we bomb hospitals in the North

It's because the milk trains coming into New Jersey hit the right switches every day that the best Vietnamese men are cut in two by American bullets that follow each other like freight cars

This is what it's like to send firebombs down from air-conditioned cockpits.

This is what it's like to be told to fire into a reed hut with an automatic weapon.

It's because we have new packaging for smoked oysters that bomb holes appear in the rice paddies

It is because we have so few women sobbing in back rooms,
because we have so few children's heads torn apart by high-velocity bullets,
because we have so few tears falling on our own hands
that the Super Sabre turns and screams down toward the earth.

It's because taxpayers move to the suburbs that we transfer populations. The Marines use cigarette lighters to light the thatched roofs of huts because so many Americans own their own homes.

IV

I see a car rolling toward a rock wall.
The treads in the face begin to crack.
We all feel like tires being run down roads under heavy cars.

The teen-ager imagines herself floating through the Seven Spheres.
Oven doors are found
open.
Soot collects over the doorframe, has children, takes courses,
goes mad, and dies.

There is a black silo inside our bodies, revolving fast.
Bits of black paint are flaking off,
where the motorcycles roar, around and around,
rising higher on the silo walls,
the bodies bent toward the horizon,
driven by angry women dressed in black.

*   *   *

I know that books are tired of us.
I *know* they are chaining the Bible to chairs.
Books don't want to remain in the same room with us anymore.

New Testaments are escaping . . . dressed as women . . . they go off
    after dark.
And Plato! Plato . . . Plato wants to go backwards. . . .
He wants to hurry back up the river of time, so he can end as some
    blob of sea flesh rotting on an Australian beach.

V

Why are they dying? I have written this so many times.
They are dying because the President has opened a Bible again.
They are dying because gold deposits have been found among the
    Shoshoni Indians.

They are dying because money follows intellect!
And intellect is like a fan opening in the wind—

The Marines think that unless they die the rivers will not move.
They are dying so that the mountain shadows will continue to fall east
      in the afternoon,
so that the beetle can move along the ground near the fallen twigs.

VI

But if one of those children came near that we have set on fire,
came toward you like a gray barn, walking,
you would howl like a wind tunnel in a hurricane,
you would tear at your shirt with blue hands,
you would drive over your own child's wagon trying to back up,
the pupils of your eyes would go wild—

If a child came by burning, you would dance on a lawn,
trying to leap into the air, digging into your cheeks,
you would ram your head against the wall of your bedroom
like a bull penned too long in his moody pen—

If one of those children came toward me with both hands
in the air, fire rising along both elbows,
I would suddenly go back to my animal brain,
I would drop on all fours, screaming,
my vocal chords would turn blue, so would yours,
it would be two days before I could play with my own children again.

VII

I want to sleep awhile in the rays of the sun slanting over the snow.
Don't wake me.
Don't tell me how much grief there is in the leaf with its natural oils.
Don't tell me how many children have been born with stumpy hands
      all those years we lived in St. Augustine's shadow.

Tell me about the dust that falls from the yellow daffodil shaken in the
	restless winds.
Tell me about the particles of Babylonian thought that still pass
	through the earthworm every day.
Don't tell me about "the frightening laborers who do not read books."

Now the whole nation starts to whirl,
the end of the Republic breaks off,
Europe comes to take revenge,
the mad beast covered with European hair rushes through the mesa
	bushes in Mendocino County,
pigs rush toward the cliff,
the waters underneath part: in one ocean luminous globes float up (in
	them hairy and ecstatic men—)
in the other, the teeth mother, naked at last.

Let us drive cars
up
the light beams
to the stars . . .

And return to earth crouched inside the drop of sweat
that falls
from the chin of the Protestant tied in the fire.

II

All around me men are working,
but I am stubborn, and take no part.
The main difference is this:
I prize the breasts of the Mother.

TAO TE CHING

I came out of the Mother naked,
and I will be naked when I return.
The Mother gave, and the Mother takes away,
I love the Mother.

OLD TESTAMENT, *restored*

I Came Out of the Mother Naked

1

I know the poet is not supposed to talk to the reader in the middle of his book. We're supposed to communicate only through the dream-voice of the poem. But I often long for some prose when I'm reading a book of poems. So I'm going to set down here some ideas about Great Mother culture, and drop a poem in now and then.

When the *Tao Te Ching* talks of the growth of ecstatic life as "the Return," the implication is that each man was once with the Mother—having gone out into masculine consciousness, a man's job is to return.

The Swiss scholar Bachofen suggested for the first time in his book *Mother Right,* published in 1861, the idea, embarrassing to the Swiss, that in every past society known a matriarchy has preceded the present patriarchy. His evidence, drawn from Mediterranean sources, was massive. Just as every adult was once inside the mother, every society was once inside the Great Mother. In Greece this mother absorption lasted until maybe 2000 B.C. What we call masculine consciousness is a very recent creation.

Men prefer to remember back only to that point in culture when they took over. Freud could only imagine a great father running the primal horde. But archaeologists have found hundreds of statues in caves and settlement ruins during the last thirty years going back many centuries, and they have never found a statue of the Great Father—the statues found, all over the world, are statues of the Mother.

Because men prefer not to remember the thousands and thousands of years in which the Great Mother had total power, almost no one has discussed what we could call "the Change." If it is true that mother consciousness preceded father consciousness, then two further things follow: women at some time must have had immense power, running all areas of life: law, agriculture, division of wealth, social custom, and especially religion. There must have been a war, probably dramatic and long-drawn-out. Surely the Great Mother did not give in to men willingly: she must have fought against the growth of masculine consciousness and father gods, and the men in turn must have fought for centuries against the Great Mother, burning her temples and killing her priests, while shamans dressed as women struggled hard to absorb her magical power, castrated priests to absorb her religious power, wigged judges to absorb her judicial power.

Beowulf I think describes the destruction of Great Mother culture in northern Europe; it is a historical poem, and perhaps three thousand years of fighting are summed up in it. Grendel, "the son," stands for all the priests of the Mother; and when they are killed, the hero has to face the Mother herself. Jung (so far as I know) did not comment on *Beowulf*, but he unraveled the Andromeda dragon fight, and from it deduced that the hero mythology of ancient Greece describes a centuries-long fight against the Mothers. At one time, all men were within "the Great Mother circle" and could not get out. To attempt and win the dragon fight is the same thing as to achieve masculine consciousness, and get out of the circle. The dragon in inner life is man's fear of women, and in public life, it is the matriarchy's conservative energy. Perseus, "the Destroyer," defeated both Medusa and a dragon; Theseus attacked a mother-monster at the center of the labyrinth and, with the help of a thread given to him by a woman hostile to the Great Mother, got back out. Hansel is a hero; with the help of Gretel, he put the Great Mother into her own oven. A "hero" is a man who succeeded in achieving even a slight amount of masculine consciousness. All men remembered it.

Intuitive gifts are being given. We can now understand stories that readers of classical literature have wanted to understand for centuries and could not. Mysteriously, knowledge denied to the conscious mind for several thousand years seeps up, it wells from the ground, beginning in the nineteenth century as men felt a curious longing to dig down, first into the earth around the Mediterranean, then into the earth of the psyche.

When reading many old stories, we have to learn to change pronouns. For example, it is not a male giant but a woman who says, "I smell a man!" When men took over, they did their best to suppress all memories of the hostile mothers, and the long age of woman power: the change of pronouns was more a wish than an act. But evidently much of the literature written under the Mother has been destroyed. The Sanskrit and Chinese civilizations certainly destroyed, rather than rewrote: there are reports of the ancient Chinese burning a hundred thousand books in a day. Only what was in memory remained: astrology, the great intellectual triumph of the Mother civilization, is left, the Tarot psychology, the *I Ching*, and fairy tales all over the world. In some cultures, the men rewrote literature instead of destroying it. There is Mother literature visible behind many stories and poems in the Old Testament. For example, here is a lovely quatrain in the King James *Job*:

> *I came out of the mother naked,*
> *and I will be naked when I return.*
> *The Lord gave, and the Lord takes away,*
> *Blessed be the name of the Lord.*

But the disunity of the images makes it clear that the poem once went this way:

> *I came out of the Mother naked,*
> *and I will be naked when I return.*
> *The Mother gave, and the Mother takes away,*
> *I love the Mother.*

2

We have then inside us two worlds of consciousness: one world associated with the dark, and one world with the light. Surely this double consciousness is precisely what the yin-yang circle of the Chinese describes. The dark half corresponds to the consciousness developed in the matriarchies, the white to the consciousness developed in the patriarchies that followed. The Chinese had passed out of the Mother phase perhaps two thousand years before the Jews and Greeks made their way out (supposing that the Greek's dragon fight took place around 2000 B.C.). The yin-yang circle is the hope of a balanced consciousness. What they called "yin," I will call here mother consciousness or feminine consciousness; yang, father or masculine consciousness.

Mother consciousness was in the world first, and embodied itself century after century in its favorite images: the night, the sea, animals with curving horns and cleft hooves, the moon, bundles of grain. Four favorite creatures of the Mother were the turtle, the owl, the dove, and the oyster—all womb-shaped, night, or ancient round sea creatures. Matriarchy thinking is intuitive and moves by associative leaps. Bachofen discovered that it favored the left side (the feeling side) of the body. When the Nicene Creed says Christ sits on the right hand of God, you know you are in a patriarchy.

When masculine consciousness became aware of itself, it took for its main image the bright blue sky surrounding the sun—its metal then was gold: Apollo had gold sun rays around his head. The right hand became favored over the left, mountaintops over valleys, one and three over two and four, the square over the circle. It creates straight roads. Matriarchies are interested primarily in what is inside walls, but the patriarchies become aware of the space between walls; empires grow from patriarchies. The patriarchs plot out the ground in huge squares. In thinking, Socrates sounds the note: avoid myths—which are always stories of the Mother anyway—and think logically, in a straight line. Patriarchies develop the thinking power of the newest part of the brain, the neo-cortex; the Great Mother may be considered the goddess of the cortex, or mammal brain. The mother goddesses of Crete were always sculpted with their breasts bare, as if to say: I have breasts, therefore I am. Father consciousness tries to control mammal nature through rules, morality, commandments, and tries to reach the spirit through asceticism. The Chinese describe it as the cold, the clear, the south side of the mountain (on which the light always falls), the north side of the river (always in sunlight), the rational, the spirit, the hard.

In mother consciousness there is affection for nature, compassion, love of water, grief and care for the dead, love of whatever is hidden, intuition, ecstasy. The Chinese describe it as the north side of the mountain (always in shadow) and the south side of the river (always in shadow); also as the valley of the world.

3

Before the white people came, Drinks Water, an old Dakota holy man, dreamed that the Indians would be defeated, and warned that when that happened, they would have to live in square houses. Black Elk mentions this in *Black Elk Speaks,* taken down in 1931. He was living then in a square house, and said, "It is a bad way to live, for there can be no power in a square. You have noticed that everything an Indian does is in a circle, and that is because the Power of the World always works in circles, and everything tries to be round. In the old days we were a strong and happy people, all our power came to us from the sacred hoop of the nation. . . . Everything the Power of the World does is done in a circle. . . . The wind, in its greatest power, whirls. Birds make their nests in circles, for theirs is the same religion as ours. . . . Our teepees were round like the nests of birds, and these were always set in a circle. . . . But the Wasichus have put us in these square houses. Our power is gone and we are dying. . . ."

The American ethnologist Lewis Henry Morgan understood that the Iroquois nation was a matriarchy, and described it as such in 1851. This description of a living matriarchy surprised Bachofen, and pleased him. The American ground, with so much mother consciousness in it, had been invaded by Puritans, fanatic father types. They painted all their churches white, inside and out, and lived in a square. They cared nothing for mammals; steamboats floated down the Missouri carrying nothing but buffalo tongues.

Father consciousness at its highest, when it does not reject the spiritual mother, is intense, spiritual, glowing. When it is crude, it sounds like this (a passage written by two white men in 1864):

Again we come to the great law of right. The white race stood upon this undeveloped continent ready and willing to execute the Divine injunction, to replenish the earth and *subdue* it. The savage races in possession, either refused or imperfectly obeyed the first law of the Creator. On the one side stood the white race in the command of God, armed with his law; on the other, the savage, resisting the execution of that law. The result could not be evaded by any human device. God's law will ever triumph, even through the imperfect instrumentality of human agency. In the case before us, the Indian races were in the wrongful possession of a continent required by the superior right of the white man. This right, founded in the wisdom of God, eliminated by the ever-operative law of progress, will continue to assert its dominion, with varying success, contingent on the use of means employed, until all opposition is hushed in the perfect reign of the superior aggressive principle.

—*A History of the Great Massacre, by the Sioux Indians in Minnesota,* by Charles S. Bryant and Abel Much (Cincinnati: Rickey and Carroll, 1864)

4

The earliest sculptures unearthed in Ice Age caves (Venus of Willendorf, for example) are statues of a Great Mother, breasts and hips immense to suggest her abundance. This mother, who brings to birth and nourishes what is born, we could call the Good Mother. She loves children, rams, rabbits, fish, bulls, all infant things, all things capable of giving birth. All the vegetation mothers, the Demeter and Isis mothers, share in this energy. The oven is her womb inside the house; in matriarchies, only women are allowed to use it. Her image is the joyful spiral, the cornucopia on the Thanksgiving table full of pumpkins (though the Puritans did not understand that); she is the seashell, old men hear the sea in her. The ancients usually sculpted her sitting, holding a child in her lap, in her thirties. Her colors are russet and brown; hearths, ovens, and water jars are statues of her. She likes men, though she treats them as children. She threatens no one. She is called "good" because she wants everything now alive to remain alive.

The trouble is that a society cannot have one of the Mothers without having all of them. When a culture begins to return to the Mother, each person in the culture begins to descend, layer after layer, into his

A Good Mother (Egyptian)

A Death Mother (Huastec)—worked into the back of a Quetzalcoatl statue

own psyche. When he starts to go down, the dead are grateful, and the trees and plants stir as if waking. As he sinks away from the Father's house, he may see, even before he sees the Good Mother, the Death Mother, and become aware that people die for other reasons than that they grow old. When the motion was going the other way, when men were moving away from the Mother, the first mother they stopped drawing or painting was the Death Mother. She never appears in Christian iconography: the Christians kept only a merciful Mother. Lilith appears seldom in the Old Testament. Hecuba was the last reminder of the Death Mother in Demeter civilization. The Indian subcontinent, by contrast, never left the Mother, and their Death Mother, Kali, still has active temples in India. Lorca's work resonates with the tremendous energy of the Death Mother; he distinguished between certain works of imagination by whether she was present or not. He noticed her presence particularly in flamenco dancing, and *cante hondo* guitar, and when she was there, he said the imagination had *duende,* and he loved that. The Death Mother is usually portrayed with her tongue stiff and poking out, to indicate that she has absorbed masculine power as well as all chthonic feminine power. She is not feeble like "Father Time." Kali is often sculpted dancing on a dead man, skulls like love beads around her neck. The Mexican Death Mother Coatlicue wears a skirt made of Mother Goddess snakes. The Death Mother in Scandinavia, visible worked into silver on the outside of the Gundestrup Cauldron, wore a band across the forehead, with hair falling away to each side—and no doubt robes with sickle moons on them and owls. She is remembered in fairy tales as "the evil witch." And she stands for black magic, just as the Good Mother stands for white magic.

If we draw a vertical line on a page, to represent the life-death line, we can then draw in an immense circle at the top for the Good Mother, and at the bottom another circle for the Death Mother. The Death Mother's job is to end everything the Good Mother has brought to birth.

Keats came close to her:

I met a lady in the meads
Full beautiful, a fairy's child;
Her hair was long, her foot was light,
And her eyes were wild. . . .

She took me to her elfin grot,
And there she gaz'd and sighed full sore,
And there I shut her wild wild eyes
With kisses four.

And there she lullèd me asleep,
And there I dream'd, ah woe betide,
The latest dream I ever dream'd
On the cold hill side.

I saw pale kings, and princes too,
Pale warriors, death pale were they all;
They cry'd, "La belle dame sans merci
Hath thee in thrall!"

I saw their starv'd lips in the gloam
With horrid warning gapèd wide,
And I awoke, and found me here
On the cold hill side.

And this is why I sojourn here
Alone and palely loitering,
Though the sedge is wither'd from the lake,
And no birds sing.

Keats turned back to the Mother (there were no "Romantic" poets in "classical" Greece, because they were moving away from the Mother), and he went far back alone, very close to her. To his surprise, the Mother he found turned out to be a Death Mother. Yet he was content. It is father consciousness that is terrified of death, not being sure that the white spark will survive. Mother consciousness is more confident that the thread of sparks will remain unbroken.

5

Most students of the matriarchies accept the idea that we can distinguish in the Great Mother a Good Mother and a Death Mother.

Graves accepts it. But Erich Neumann in his marvelous book *The Great Mother* makes an astonishing suggestion. He suggests that there is another arm, that there is actually a four-armed mother cross, that if we want to imagine Mother Energy as the ancients did, we must add another arm crossing the life-death line.

On this line, the plane of mental and spiritual life, we find an abundant mother also, whom we can call the Dancing Mother or the Ecstatic Mother. We can draw a circle for her on the "east" side of the cross. We can imagine each Mother as a magnetic force field. The Ecstatic Mother tends to intensify mental and spiritual life until it reaches ecstasy. She was sculpted almost always dancing, and in her teens or twenties, to distinguish her from the Good Mother. She is associated with the out-of-doors, with fields not yet domesticated, just as the Good Mother is associated with the fireplace. When a man has been alone for many hours or days outdoors, he can sometimes feel the Ecstatic Mother enter—or rather, he accepts her radiation at last. One of her oldest names in Greece was the Muse, and both men and women know that without her energy, their poems will be flat and thick-kneed. Most dancers are on the Ecstatic Mother's plane. Isadora Duncan sometimes stunned audiences—evidently when she danced, they had the impression they were seeing the Ecstatic Mother. Artemis and all the dancing mothers, all the virgin mothers, and all the visionary mothers, Diotima and Sophia, share the energy of this field. She was often called "Virgin," not because she avoided sexual joy, but because her main job was not to bring children into the world, but to bring ecstasy into the world.

When a man or woman is joyful alone, the Ecstatic Mother is there. If a person is "alienated," like Beckett, or cannot bear to be alone, one of the other Mothers is there. But if a man has no money or friends, and the Ecstatic Mother comes, then, as Thoreau said, he needs nothing more. He can never have too much of that solitude. Leonardo had almost no relationship with his own parents, nor evidently with other people, but he had a constant relationship with a spiritual parent, the Ecstatic Mother. She visited him always, and he did several paintings of her, showing over her shoulder the wild rocks where she lived. Several years ago, before I had read of the Ecstatic Mother, I wrote a prose poem on one of his paintings of her, *The Virgin and St. Anne* in the Louvre:

Leonardo's Secret

The Virgin is thinking of a child—who will drive the rioters out of the temple—and her face is smiling. Her smile is full, it reminds you of a cow's side, or a stubble field with water standing in it.

Behind her head, jagged blue rocks. The jagged rocks slope up quietly, and fall back, washed by a blue light, like the light in an octopus's eyes. The rocks, though no one is there, are not empty of people.

The rocks have not been forgotten by the sea either. They are the old brains of the sea. They glow for several seconds every morning as the old man who lives in a hut on the shore drinks down his glass of salt water.

All of my poems come from the Ecstatic Mother; everyone's poems do. Men in patriarchies try to deny the truth that all creativity lies in feminine consciousness; it is part of the fight with the Mother. But if the Mothers are immense force fields, then men are receiving magnets, who fly about in inner space. The masculine soul in a woman is pulled in a similar way.

We have talked of the poles of the Mother as if they could be drawn on a page; we must try to imagine those poles in three-dimensional space. Powerful force fields walk all around us. A woman radiates her energy whether she wants to or not; she has it from birth. But a man's spiritual life, as we know, is full of curious accidents. If he meets an Ecstatic Mother either in the eternal world or in this one, he will be pulled toward poetry and ecstasy. Dante met an Ecstatic Mother, whom he called Beatrice, when he was nine and she was nine; he describes it in *La Vita Nuova* (The New Life).

All men's poems are written by men already flying toward the Ecstatic Mother. It's possible for a poem to talk about the Death Mother, but I think the energy that brings the words alive belongs to the Ecstatic Mother. The father poets, like Pope, try to find a substitute for the Ecstatic Mother inside male consciousness; their poems have excitement but no ecstasy. However, they live a long time.

The Ecstatic Mother, then, is the abundant mother on the spiritual plane. What shall we call her opposite, the force field waiting at the other end of that arm? For this Mother the Greek matriarchies always used the mask of Medusa. Living snakes rose from her head, to suggest the fantastic concentration of Great Mother energy she contained; and it was said that if a man looked into her eyes he turned to stone. In other words, the concentration of Great Mother energy was so great that it stopped the developing masculine consciousness in its tracks. The male ends either as stone, or as a mirror-personality like Narcissus.

Any concentration of Great Mother consciousness is dangerous. It is possible that "angels" mask in a patriarchy memories of such mother intensities. Rilke in the marvelous opening of his *Duino Elegies* asks what would happen today if a man met an "angel." He would "fade in the strength of his (her) stronger existence." "Every angel is terrifying."

The Stone Mother perhaps represents in history the Mother culture during the time it was implacably hostile to masculine consciousness.

Whenever a man enters the force field of a Mother, he feels himself being pulled toward mothers and childhood, back toward the womb, but this time he feels himself being pulled *through* the womb, into the black nothing before life, into a countryside of black plants where he will lose all consciousness, both mother and father. The teeth in the vagina strip him as he goes through. He is dismembered while still alive. The job of this Mother is to end the intensification of mental life that the Ecstatic Mother began, to end ecstasy and spiritual growth. The alcoholic has seen the Stone Mother, and he drinks to dull the fear that his inner rivers will turn to stone. He avoids looking at the Mother, and the alcohol turns him to stone. The Stone Mother stands for numbness, paralysis, catatonia, being totally spaced out, the psyche torn to bits, arms and legs thrown all over. America's fate is to face this Mother before other industrial nations; Poe's "Descent into the Maelstrom" suggests the horror of the descent. My Lai is partway down; hard drugs that leave the boy-man permanently "stoned" are among the weapons of this Mother.

The idea of the Stone Mother helps to understand Holderlin's life. He grasped from reading ancient poetry that the Ecstatic Mother was actually alive, and not just a literary invention. Then he met a partial embodiment of her in Susette Gontard, whom he called, strangely, "Diotima." He started to move along that plane, and moved closer and closer to her, so close that he actually started writing in the ecstatic meters of the dancing Greek poets, unused for centuries. But he was only a European, part of a culture that had not taken the Ecstatic Mother seriously for a thousand years. The road toward her is glassy. He lost his footing, and was pulled in a fraction of a second into the Stone Mother's house. He became "insane," and lived quietly there, above a carpenter's shop, with the Stone Mother, for the last thirty-six years of his life.

In some cultures she is called the Teeth Mother. The intent is the same—to suggest the end of psychic life, the dismembering of the psyche. The South Asian cultures imagined the teeth on the face, but the American Indian culture and the Roman culture preferred to put the teeth in the vagina. *Sun Chief,* the Hopi autobiography, has a good Teeth Mother story. Jarrold Ramsey recently worked into English some wonderful vagina teeth poems belonging to the Paiutes; his poem is in *Alcheringa* I. Putting the teeth on the face is more accurate in some ways, since the Teeth Mother is dangerous to women as well as to men. "Little Red Riding Hood" describes a young girl being eaten by a Teeth Mother, presumably her own mother.

This teeth imagery began to surface in America about two decades ago. I first noticed the Teeth Mother in American art in de Koonings' portraits of women he did in the fifties. He saw her clearly, and did a series of portraits of her, as clear as Leonardo's in their way. A number of Vietnam veterans have come home in the last few years with tales of Vietnamese women who are said to have had razor blades inserted "surgically" into their vaginas. This is a good Teeth Mother story, adapted to medical advances.

Certain men in Europe in the early nineteenth century began to move back toward the Mother, alone. In the United States the return to the Mother as a mass movement began in the late fifties. The movement assumed, in the usual way of patriarchies, that the only Mothers in the universe were the Good Mother and the Ecstatic Mother, and that only the fathers were "evil." Half the population still show their nearness to these Mothers by their beads and long hair and ecstasy, by loving rock music, swaying back and forth half the afternoon. Woodstock was a Good Mother gathering. But the Stone and Death Mothers are standing right next to the Ecstatic Mothers. There was a hint of that at Altamont, where the Stones found themselves playing death and catatonia music. The picture we have of "Consciousness III" is patriarchal, with the dangerous mothers, as usual, invisible. But the Vietnam war has helped everyone to see how much of the Teeth Mother there is in the United States. The culture of affluence opens the psyche to the Teeth Mother and the Death Mother in ways that no one understands. Ed Sanders writes about some of that terror in his book on Charles Manson. Americans don't "believe" in the Death Mother or the Teeth Mother, but are just beginning to experience the terror of them.

6

I have brought two separate ideas into this prose: the theory that power was first held by women, that matriarchies only gradually gave way to patriarchies, is Bachofen's idea, not accepted by all anthropologists, but supported by an amazing number of recent archaeological finds, and by experiences like Malinowski's among living ancient cultures. The second idea—that the Great Mother can best be understood as a union of four "force fields"—is a completely separate concept, and in modern thinking very young. I may have mistaken the nature of the fields, or their relation to each other. And yet some sort of division was clearly made in ancient times, and insisted on.

Men's fear of women seems to be a fundamental emotion on this planet. It is rarely talked about, and in the U.S. it is getting worse. It is possible that when a culture refuses to visualize the dangerous mothers, men then become vaguely afraid of all women, and finally of the entire feminine side of their own personalities. That is a disaster.

Ancient civilizations visualized the dangerous mothers precisely to save human beings from disaster. Ancient poems spoke freely of fear of the Mothers and of women. In Rilke's powerful poem on the fear of women—set down here in my own translation—he goes back to an old Egyptian saying:

"We Must Die Because We Have Known Them"

Papyrus Prisse. From the sayings
of Ptah-hotep, manuscript from 2000 B.C.

"We must die because we have known them." Die
of the unbelievable flower of their smile. Die
of their delicate hands. Die
of women.

Let the boy praise the death-givers
when they float magnificently through his
heart-halls. From his blossoming body
he cries to them:
impossible to reach. Oh, how strange they are.
They go swiftly over
the peaks of his feelings and pour down the night
marvelously altered into his deserted
arm-valley. The wind that rises
in their dawn makes his body leaves rustle. His brooks
glisten away.

And it's right that the grown man
shivers and remains silent. The man
who has blundered around all night
on the mountains of his feelings
remains silent.
As the old sailor remains silent
and the terrors
he's experienced leap about in him as if in rocking cages.

The ancients also took the force field of the Mothers and stretched them out into narratives—myths or fairy tales we call them; also they put on robes and pretended to be the Mothers themselves. A tragedy after all is a play in which the secret principles of the dangerous mothers take hold of the actors. The sight of the Death Mother and the Stone Mother walking around on stage was so terrifying to men that Aristotle described its chief effect as "catharsis," "purgation"—it cleaned a man out for days. It also increased the desire to "know." And if a man wished to know more of the Mothers, he could always join one of the Mysteries, invariably linked with a Great Mother shrine, such

An Ecstatic Mother (*Mycenean*)

A Teeth Mother (Balinese)—Mask

as the shrine of Diana at Ephesus. What was taught in the Mysteries about the Mother is lost.

The more one studies ancient cultures of the Mediterranean the greater the admiration one has for their fantastic powers of visualization. The psychic rulers of Mycenae and Crete evidently used architecture to teach inward things—that is, they built a labyrinth, with vagina-like passages, and a wild bull at the center, pawing the ground, to represent the Mother, torn-off arms and legs scattered about. Apparently boys and girls during "initiation ceremonies" would be conducted inside.

The visualizations surely helped women to understand the sense of power that they feel in themselves, but which no modern metaphors explain. And it helped women to understand the risks of their development. If we return to the four-leafed mother cross—the same shape as the Celtic cross—we see it's possible that a woman's psyche grows by moving out along one of the two arms—in both directions perhaps, but on only one of the arms: a woman like a man apparently lives primarily either on the life-death line or the spiritual line. I've mentioned that dancers often live on the Ecstatic Mother's plane, and Scorpios have links with the Death Mother, etc.

The farther a woman goes out on the end of an arm, the more power she has. That power is for good and power for evil. It is also power over weather, over plant growth, and power to cause transformations. Girls in the Middle West often decide to stay at the center of the cross, where they will be safe. That strange passive quality in so many American women comes from that decision. A woman's problem is that if she does leave the center, and go farther out, which Mother will she find there? Whichever she finds she will become, for she is that one already. Many women in a patriarchal society then elect to remain near the center; but if they do that, their spiritual growth stops, and they die, spiritually. If a Scorpio, for example, forbids her radiation to go out, the rays will turn back on her, and turn her to stone.

Western literature since Socrates basically describes men's escape from the Mother, and women get little help from it, as Anaïs Nin mentions in her diaries. Most of the literature written in the last two thousand years has been written by men about their growth, which is exciting precisely because it is so late coming. Neumann believes that a few tales have survived, among them "Amor and Psyche" from *The Golden Ass*, embodying ideas of women's growth, but there are few. Men cannot easily visualize woman's "road" of growth, and women have for centuries stopped trying to do so themselves. Doris Lessing, though, along with a handful of others, is returning to this interrupted labor.

The increasing strength of poetry, defense of earth, and mother consciousness, implies that after hundreds of years of being motionless, the Great Mother is moving again in the psyche. Every day her face becomes clearer. We are becoming more sensitive, more open to her influence. She is returning, or we are returning to her; everyone who looks down into his own psyche sees her, just as in leaves floating on a pond you can sometimes make out faces. The pendulum is just now turning away from the high point of father consciousness and starting to sweep down. The pendulum rushes down, the Mothers rush toward us, we can all feel the motion downward, the speed increasing.

7

I don't expect these ideas to help writers write better poems, nor should anyone examine my own poems for evidence of them, for most of my poems were written without benefit of them. As for women, this essay will not tell women much about themselves that they don't know. The division of the Mothers was evidently made by women themselves during the matriarchies, when they had all religious and myth-making power, so I don't expect it will be news to them.

The reader will not get a genuine sense of mother consciousness from reading my prose either, because I write of mother consciousness using a great deal of father consciousness. But there is no other possibility for a man. A man's father consciousness cannot be eradicated. If he tries that, he will lose everything. All he can hope to do is to join his father consciousness and his mother consciousness so as to experience what is beyond the father veil.

Right now we long to say that father consciousness is bad, and mother consciousness is good. But we know it is father consciousness saying that; it insists on putting labels on things. They are both good.

The Greeks and the Jews were right to pull away from the Mother and drive on into father consciousness; and their forward movement gave both cultures a marvelous luminosity. But now the turn has come. Women want more masculine consciousness, and men want more mother consciousness; they want a balanced consciousness. Women were not satisfied with Great Mother consciousness; if they had been, Theseus' "sister" and Hansel's "sister" would never have helped the "heroes" to destroy Mother culture.

In Mother culture, I am a student. I believe Blake when he warns us how much more we need to see:

> Now I a fourfold vision see,
> And a fourfold vision is given to me;
> 'Tis fourfold in my supreme delight
> And threefold in soft Beulah's night
> And twofold always. May God us keep
> From Single vision & Newton's sleep!

8

What all this speculation by Neumann and Esther Harding and so many contemporary poets amounts to is a revaluation of the anima, the feminine soul, following centuries of depreciation of it. All my clumsy prose amounts to is praise of the feminine soul, whether that soul appears in men or in women. The masculine soul, which in its middle range is logic and fairness, and at its highest vibrations hurries toward the spirit, also needs praise, but I am not doing that here. Here I want to do something else. We know that the despising of the feminine soul has been the cause of some of our greatest errors and disasters.

I think the reason this psychic archaeology means so much to me is that I come from Norwegian immigrants, here only three generations; in other words I come from the patriarchal and Protestant heritage of northern Europe, which is spiritually an empty ruin. Jung, whose father was a Protestant minister, said: "The intellect has achieved the most tremendous things, but all that time our spiritual house has been falling to pieces. . . . Meaning has left most religious images. . . . And I am convinced that this growing impoverishment of symbols has a meaning. . . . And if we hide our nakedness, as the Theosophists do, by putting on the gorgeous robes and trappings of the East, we are essentially lying about our own history. It would be far better simply to admit our spiritual poverty. . . . The spirit has come down from its fiery high places . . . but when spirit becomes heavy, it turns to water. . . . Therefore the way of the soul in search of its lost father . . . leads to the water, to the dark mirror that lies at the bottom. Whoever has decided to move toward the state of spiritual poverty . . . goes the way of the soul that leads to the water."

I see in my own poems and the poems of so many other poets alive now fundamental attempts to right our own spiritual balance, by encouraging those parts in us that are linked with music, with solitude, water, and trees, the parts that grow when we are far from the centers of ambition.

III

Sleepers Joining Hands

A Long Poem

The Shadow Goes Away

The woman chained to the shore stands bewildered as night comes
I don't want to wake up in the weeds, and find the light
gone out in the body, and the cells dark. . . .
I see the cold ocean rise to take us
as I stand without feathers on the shore
and watch the blood-colored moon gobbling up the sand. . . .

The owl senses someone in the hole of his tree,
and lands with wings closing, claws out. . . .

I fall asleep, and dream I am working in the fields. . . .
Now I show the father the coat stained with goat's blood. . . .
The shadow goes away,
we are left alone in the father's house.
I knew that. . . . I sent my brother away.
I saw him turn and leave. It was a schoolyard.
I gave him to the dark people passing.
He learned to sleep alone on the high buttes.
I heard he was near the Missouri, taken in by traveling Sioux.
They taught him to wear his hair long,
to glide about naked, drinking water from his hands,
to tether horses, follow the faint trail through bent grasses. . . .

Men bound my shadow. That was in high school.
They tied it to a tree, I saw it being led away.
I dreamt that I sat in a big chair,
and every other second I disappeared.
This was during Stanley's visit to Africa.

In high school I was alone, asleep in the Law.
I slipped off one night into the water,
    swam to shore with no one watching,
left my brother alone on the ship!
On 66th Street I noticed he was gone.
I sat down and wept.
Hairs of depression come up through the palm laid on the ground,
little impulses shoot up in the dark,
in the dark the sleeping marmoset opens his eyes.
There are nights in which everything is torn
away, all piers gone. . . .
I walk through the trees, and come into the Indian encampment.
The Sioux are struggling up the mountain in disordered lines,
the field littered with robes, dogbones, thongs,
the great cooking iron in which my shadow was boiling!

Walking through the camp, I notice an old chest of drawers.
I open a drawer and see small white horses gallop away toward the back.
I see the birds inside me,
with massive shoulders, like humpbacked Puritan ministers,
a headstrong beak ahead,
and wings supple as the stingray's,
ending in claws, lifting over the shadowy peaks.

Looking down, I see dark marks on my shirt.
My mother gave me that shirt, and hoped that her son would be the
    one man in the world
who would have a happy marriage,
but look at me now—
I have been divorced five hundred times,
six hundred times yesterday alone.

I hear the sound of hoofs . . . coming. . . . Now the men
move in, smashing and burning. The huts
of the Shadowy People are turned over, the wood
utensils broken, straw mats set on fire,
digging sticks jumped on, clay bowls
smashed with dropped stones. . . .

Thousands of men come,
like dwarf antelopes in long streaming herds,
or hair flying behind the skidding racer. . . .

No ministers or teachers come out,
I am flying over my bed alone. . . .
I am flying over the Josephine forests, where only the rat builds his nest
      of leaves,
and keeps his mistress in the white dusk. . . .

The moon swims through the clogging veins,
the sun leaps from its dying bed,
divorced men and women drown in the paling, reddening sea.

The Marines turn to me. They offer me money.
I turn and leave. The sun sinks toward the darkening hills.
My mother's bed looms up in the dark.
The noose tightens,
servants of the armor brain, terrified hired men whom the sharks feed,
scales everywhere, "glittering on their bodies as they fall."

The Sea of Tranquility scattered with dead rocks,
and black dust resembling diesel oil.
The suppressed race returns: snakes and transistors filling the beaches,
pilots in armored cockpits finding their way home through moonlit
      clouds.

Meeting the Man Who Warns Me

I wake and find myself in the woods, far from the castle.
The train hurtles through lonely Louisiana at night.
The sleeper turns to the wall, delicate
aircraft dive toward earth.

A woman whispers to me, urges me to speak truths.
"I am afraid that you won't be honest with me."
Half or more of the moon rolls on in shadow.
Owls talk at night, loons wheel cries through lower waters,
fragments of the mother lie open in all low places.

I have been alone two days, and still everything is cloudy.
The body surrounds me on all sides.
I walk out and return.
Rain dripping from pine boughs, boards soaked on porches,
gray water awakens, fish slide away underneath.
I fall asleep. I meet a man from a milder planet.
I say to him: "I know Christ is from your planet!"
He lifts his eyes to me with a fierce light.
He reaches out and touches me on the tip of my cock,
and I fall asleep.

I dream that the fathers are dying.
Jehovah is dying, Jesus' father is dying,
the hired man is asleep inside the oat straw.
Samson is lying on the ground with his hollow hair.

Who is this that visits us from beneath the earth?
I see the dead like great conductors
carrying electricity under the ground,
the Eskimos suddenly looking into the womb of the seal. . . .
Water shoots into the air from manhole covers,

the walker sees it astonished and falls;
before his body hits the street
he is already far down the damp steps of the Tigris,
seeing the light given off under the door by shining hair.

Something white calls to us:
it is the darkness we saw outside the cradle.
My shadow is underneath me,
floating in the dark, in his small boat bobbing among reeds.
A fireball floats in the corner of the Eskimo's house—
It is a light that comes nearer when called!
A light the spirits turn their heads for,
suddenly shining over land and sea!
I taste the heaviness of the dream,
the northern lights curve up toward the roof of my mouth.
The energy is inside us. . . .
I start toward it, and I meet an old man.
He looms up in the road, his white hair standing up:
"Who is this who is ascending the red river?
Who is this who is leaving the dark plants?"
I don't want to leave, and walk back and forth,
looking toward the old landing.

I dream that I cannot see half of my life.
I look back, it is like the blind spot in a car.
So much just beyond the reach of our eyes,
what tramples the grasses while the horses are asleep,
the hoof marks all around the cave mouth . . .
what slips in under the door at night, and lies exhausted on the floor
        in the morning.

What cannot be remembered and cannot be forgotten,
the chaff blowing about my father's feet.
And the old man cries out: "I am here.
Either talk to me about your life, or turn back."
I look from bridges at cattle grazing,

the lizard moving stiffly over the November road,
the night frogs who give out the croak of the planet turning,
the great knees of horses loyal to the earth risen in their will.
"I am the dark spirit that lives in the dark.
Each of my children is under a leaf he chose from all the leaves in the
        universe.
When I was alone, for three years, alone,
I passed under the earth through the night-water,
I was for three days inside a warm-blooded fish.
'Purity of heart is to will one thing.'
I saw the road. . . ." "Go on! Go on!"
"A whale bore me back home, we flew through the air. . . .
Then I was a boy who had never seen the sea!
It was like a King coming to his own shores.
I feel the naked touch of the knife,
I feel the wound,
this joy I love is like wounds at sea. . . ."

The Night Journey in the Cooking Pot

I was born during the night sea-journey.
I love the whale with his warm organ pipes
        in the mouse-killing waters,
I love the men who drift, asleep, for three nights in octopus waters,
the furry men gathering wood, piling the chunks by walls,
I love the snow, I need privacy as I move,
I am all alone, floating in the cooking pot
on the sea, through the night I am alone.

            *   *   *

        The crow nests high in the fir.
    Birds leap through the snowy branches,
                uttering small cries,
The mice run dragging their tails in the new-fallen snow.

        The old tree moves in the wind.
    Sitting I leap from branch to branch,
            the old man calls out,
long prayers at dawn, the deer antlers abandoned in the snow.

            *   *   *

I float on solitude as on water . . . there is a road. . . .
I felt the road first in New York, in that great room
reading Rilke in the womanless loneliness.
How marvelous the great wings sweeping along the floor,
inwardness, inwardness, inwardness,
the inward path I still walk on,
I felt the wings brushing the floors of the dark,
trailing longer wings,
the wing marks left in the delicate sand of the corridors,
the face shining far inside the mountain.

There is a certainty that makes the fingers love each other,
and makes the body give up sleep.
The animals open their mouths, and come, glad,
in a ring.
The snow begins falling.
A winter of privacy is before us,
winter privacy,
the vast halls inside the heads of animals
lie before us, the slow
breaking of day, warm blood moving, moving,
and immense pine trees.

        *   *   *

For the first time in months I love the dark.
A joy pierces into me, it arrives like a runner,
a radio signal from inside a tree trunk,
a smile spreads over the face, the eyes fall.

Someone is asleep in the back of my house.
I feel the blood galloping in the body,
the baby whirling in the womb.
Dark bodies pass by far out at the horizon,
trailing lights like flying saucers,
the shadows go by long after the bodies have passed.
Nuns with faces smoothed by prayer
peer out from holes in the earth.

The mouse goes down the tunnel where the mice-infants light the
        whole room!
I start down, after him,
I see owls with blue flames coming from the tops of their heads,
watching from firs on each side of the road,
and snow just beginning to fall.

    They broke from the house, walked in the trees, and were lost,
        slept in the earth, brooded like wells in the deep ground,
      sleeping in anguish like grain, whole, blind in the old grave.

Who is it that visits us from beneath the snow?
Something shining far down in the ice?
Deep in the mountain the sleeper is glad.
Men with large shoulders covered with furs,
eyes closed, inexplicable.
Holy ones with eyes closed,
the cracking sound in the ice under our feet,
the frozen lake marked with caribou feet . . .

Leaves slip down, falling through their own branches.
The tree becomes naked and joyful.
Leaves fall in the tomby wood.
Some men need so little, and even that I need very little.
Suddenly I love the dancers, leaping
in the dark, jumping
into the air, and the singers and dancers and leapers!
I start to sing, and rove around the floor,
singing like "a young Lioun"

I want to rise far into the piney tops

I am not going farther from you,
I am coming nearer,
green rain carries me nearer you,
I weave drunkenly about the page,
I love you,
I never knew that I loved you
until I was swallowed by the invisible,
my black shoes evaporating, rising about my head. . . .

For we are like the branch bent in the water . . .
Taken out, it is whole, it was always whole. . . .

          *   *   *

I see the road ahead,
and my body cries out, and leaps into the air,

and throws itself on the floor, knocking over the chairs.
I think I am the body,
the body rushes in and ties me up,
and then goes through the house. . . .

I am on the road, the next instant in the ditch,
    face down on the earth,
wasting energy talking to idiots.
Clumsy wings flop around the room,
I know what I must do,
I am ashamed looking at the fish in the water.

The barn doors are open. His first breath touches the manger hay
and the King a hundred miles away
stands up. He calls his ministers.
"Find him.
There cannot be two rulers in one body."
He sends his wise men out along the arteries,
along the winding tunnels, into the mountains,
to kill the child in the old moonlit villages of the brain.

                *   *   *

The mind waters run out on the rug.
Pull the mind in,
pull the arm in,
it will be taken off by a telephone post.

Suddenly I am those who run large railroads at dusk,
who stand around the fallen beast howling,
who cannot get free,
the man the lion bounding catches in the African grass.
I stop, a hand turns over in my stomach,
this is not the perfect freedom of the saints.

I decide that death is friendly.
Finally death seeps up through the tiniest capillaries of my toes.

I fall into my own hands,
    fences break down under horses,
cities starve, whole towns of singing women carrying to the burial fields
    the look I saw on my father's face,
I sit down again, I hit my own body,
I shout at myself, I see what I have betrayed.
What I have written is not good enough.
Who does it help?
I am ashamed sitting on the edge of my bed.

Water Drawn Up Into the Head

Now do you understand the men who laugh all night in their sleep?
Here is some prose:

> *Once there was a man who went to a far country*
> *to get his inheritance and then returned.*

There are places for our feet to go.

When we come face to face with you,
the holder laughs and is glad!
He laughs like the mad condor in his stickly nest!

The feminine creature at the edge of town,
men with rifles all around.
I am passive, listening to the lapping waves,
I am divine, drinking the air,
consciousness fading or sweeping out over the husky soybean fields like
     a revolving beacon all night,
horses at the end of their tethering ropes,
the wing of affection passes over,
flying bulls glimpsed passing the moon disc.

We know the world with all its visible stars,
earth, water, air, and fire,
but when alone we see that great tomb is not God.
There are spirits,
     who wheel with sparks at night in a room,
but everyone knows they are not God.
We know of Christ, who raised the dead, and started time.
He is not God, and is not called God.

When the waterholes go, and the fish
     flop about

in the caked mud, they can moisten each other faintly.
      That is good, but best
is to let them lose themselves in a river.
So rather than saying that Christ is God or he is not,
it is better to forget all that
and lose yourself in the curved energy.
I entered that energy one day,
that is why I have lived alone in old places,
that is why I have knelt in churches, weeping,
that is why I have become a stranger to my father.
We have no name for you, so we say:
he makes grass grow upon the mountains,
and gives food to the dark cattle of the sea,
he feeds the young ravens that call on him.

                    *   *   *

I have sat here alone for two hours. . . .
I have sat here alone for two years!
There is another being living inside me.
He is looking out of my eyes.
I hear him
in the wind through the bare trees.

I met the King coming through the traffic.
He said, I shall give to you more pain than wounds at sea.

That is why I am so glad in fall.
I walk out, throw my arms up, and am glad.
The thick leaves fall,
falling past their own trunk,
and the tree goes naked,
leaving only the other one.

An Extra Joyful Chorus for Those
Who Have Read This Far

I sit alone late at night.
I sit with eyes closed, thoughts shoot through me.
I am not floating, but fighting.
In the marshes the mysterious mother calls to her moor-bound chicks.
I love the Mother.
I am an enemy of the Mother, give me my sword.
I leap into her mouth full of seaweed.

I am the single splinter that shoots through the stratosphere leaving fire
        trails!
I walk upright, robes flapping at my heels,
I am fleeing along the ground like a frightened beast.
I am the ball of fire the woodman cuts out of the wolf's stomach,
I am the sun that floats over the Witch's house,
I am the horse sitting in the chestnut tree singing,
I am the man locked inside the oakwomb,
waiting for lightning, only let out on stormy nights.
I am the steelhead trout that hurries to his mountain mother,
to live again in the stream where he was born,
gobbling up the new water.

Sometimes when I read my own poems late at night,
I sense myself on a long road,
I feel the naked thing alone in the universe,
the hairy body padding in the fields at dusk. . . .

I have floated in the eternity of the cod heaven,
I have felt the silver of infinite numbers brush my side—

I am the crocodile unrolling and slashing through the mudded water,
I am the baboon crying out as her baby falls from the tree,
I am the light that makes the flax blossom at midnight!
I am an angel breaking into three parts over the Ural Mountains!
I am no one at all.

*   *   *

I am a thorn enduring in the dark sky,
I am the one whom I have never met,
I am a swift fish shooting through the troubled waters,
I am the last inheritor crying out in deserted houses
I am the salmon hidden in the pool on the temple floor
I am what remains of the beloved
I am an insect with black enamel knees hugging the curve of insanity
I am the evening light rising from the ocean plains
I am an eternal happiness fighting in the long reeds.

Our faces shine with the darkness reflected from the Tigris,
cells made by the honeybees that go on growing after death,
a room darkened with curtains made of human hair.

The panther rejoices in the gathering dark.
Hands rush toward each other through miles of space.
All the sleepers in the world join hands.